Come Out of Her My People

OR

An Answer to the questions of a Gentlewoman (a professor in the Antichristian Church of England) about Hearing the Public Ministers: where it is largely discussed and proved to be sinful and unlawful

By
JOHN LILBURNE

Published by *The Rota* at the University of Exeter
1971

BIBLIOGRAPHICAL NOTE

Come out of her my people is reproduced by permission of the Trustees of the British Museum. Shelf-mark 479.a.9. Pollard and Redgrave, *Short title catalogue*, no. 15596.

2nd Edition (Revised) 1984

Printed and bound in Great Britain by Short Run Press Ltd., Exeter

PREFATORY NOTE

John Lilburne's career began in 1637 with 'martyrdom' for the anti-episcopal cause led during the 1630s by Prynne, Burton, and Bastwick. Their pamphlet war reached its climax with *News from Ipswich* (1636, probably by Prynne) and Burton's inflammatory sermons published as *For God, and the King* (1636). Bastwick contributed his *Letany* (1637). Lilburne (?1615-1657) was introduced to Bastwick in the Gatehouse prison and offered to get the *Letany* printed in Holland. Bastwick accepted. The tract arrived in England in mid-1637 and soon afterwards Prynne, Burton and Bastwick were tried for libel in Star Chamber, found guilty and sentenced to mutilation, to the pillory and imprisonment.

Lilburne came home in December 1637. Betrayed by a confederate, he was arrested by agents of the Stationers' Company and imprisoned by the Privy Council. In January 1638, brought to the Star Chamber office, he rejected the *ex officio* oath. Justifying his refusal, Lilburne brought for the first time into Star Chamber the legal case mounted in *An Argument of Master Nicholas Fuller* (1607), to which generations of puritans had appealed in the Court of High Commission, declaring the oath both illegal under common law and contrary to the law of nature and therefore sinful. He was found guilty of contempt, pilloried and remanded until he should conform. The pillorying became an occasion for handing out copies of the *Letany* and for preaching against the bishops. Still refusing to admit his fault, Lilburne remained in the Fleet until his release three years later on Oliver Cromwell's motion in the Long Parliament. In his 'Copy of a Letter', dated November 1638, Lilburne claimed to have been converted to separatism during his punishment, 'being never yet in any of their [separate] Congregations in *England*' (pp 16-17).

While still in prison, Lilburne managed to publish pamphlets providing narratives of his sufferings. *A Worke of the Beast* (1638) includes his first published justification of separatism (pp 14-19), but *Come out of her my people* (1639) formulates the case at greater length, ostensibly to persuade an unidentified gentlewoman of the sinfulness of listening to the 'Publicke Ministers'. The title of the present pamphlet, which bears the clearest witness to Lilburne's now uncompromising separatism, is drawn from a reference in *Revelations* to the fall of Babylon: 'I heard another voice from heaven, saying, Come out of her, my people, that ye be not partakers of her sins' (18:4). 'Babylon' is a metaphor for the Church of England, and Lilburne reads his text as an injunction to God's people to adopt separatist principles. His call to 'come out' of the Babylonian church is couched in tones of apocalyptic urgency: the anti-papal exegesis of *Revelations* is unmistakeably Foxean (pp 15-18). Comparing himself with St Paul, Lilburne interprets his sufferings as those of a witness to God's cause assured of his right to speak as a one of the elect (pp 29-31).

Claiming that the bishops' calling was not *jure divino* (as the Laudians had maintained) but *jure diabolo*, Lilburne consigned the Church to 'Antichrists Kingdome' (pp 8,11). His most sustained argument in favour of the 'way of Totall Separation' depended not merely on the received notion that the Pope was Antichrist, and on the supposed popishness of the Laudian bishops, but also on the doctrine of apostolic succession underlaying the bishops' *jure divino* claims. The calling of all ministers and officials of the Church of England was similarly tainted, Lilburne continued, since each in turn derived his authority from the bishops. This was enough to invalidate their ministry. Invoking the commonplace distinction between the person and his office or calling, Lilburne inferred that it was sinful to hear the bishops' sermons whether or not they were in themselves good men (pp 8-13). Preaching the 'outside' of the Word, they remained ignorant of the 'marrow and pith of it', since their understandings were clouded by the 'Foggie Mists of the darke and black Kingdome' (p 10). The true Christian was therefore obliged to separate from communion with the Church.

Lilburne challenged Laud to public debate, intimating that the bishops' case rested solely on 'Clubb Law' (pp 32-35). Even so, adopting the conventional puritan affirmation of the principle of non-resistance, he denied that his opposition to episcopacy amounted to rebellion. He argues that the injunction in *Acts* to obey God rather than men nevertheless requires the believer to submit passively to the civil magistrate, and adds that rebellion is never justified by oppression, temporal or spiritual (p 14). There was no anticipation here of Lilburne's subsequent espousal of resistance theory, which, in fact, he got from parliamentarian apologists in the early 1640s. *Come out of her my people* is remarkable, in view of the secularism and the position on toleration usually associated with the

Levellers, for its apocalyptic language and the righteous intolerance of the case it makes out for separatism.

Come out of her my people, reproduced by permission of the Trustees of the British Library (Shelf Mark 479.a.9; Pollard and Redgrave, *Short Title Catalogue*, no.15596), was published in 1639. Internal evidence (pp 27,31) indicates that it was written about four months after Lilburne's appearance in May before the King's Attorney and the Solicitor General. He refers to the tract in his 'Copy of a Letter' (dated November 1638 but not published until 1645 at the end of *Innocency and Truth Justified*). *Come out of her my people* appeared under Lilburne's name, but, of course, without an imprimatur. In *A Coppy of a Letter*, addressed to the wardens of the Fleet and dated 4 October 1640, Lilburne alludes to his use of a printer in Holland, noting the seizure of two thousands of his books on their way from Amsterdam (pp 4-8). *A Worke of the Beast* (1638), reprinted in W. Haller (ed), *Tracts on Liberty*, 3 vols. (New York, 1934), II, 1-34, describes Lilburne's punishment with a version of his pillory speech. *The Christian Mans Triall*, dealing with the Star Chamber episode, first published in 1638, survives only in the second edition of 1641.

Lilburne's own accounts of this part of his life are in his *Innocency and Truth Justified* (1645), pp 38-9, 72-74 and *Legall Fundamentall Liberties* (1649), pp 21-22. Bastwick's somewhat different account, published after he and Lilburne had quarrelled, is in his own *Just Defence* (1645).

The standard biography of Lilburne is P. Gregg, *Freeborn John* (London, 1961). See also W. Haller, *The Rise of Puritanism* (New York, 1938) for an account of Lilburne's early career and the bibliography of his early writings. On the probable role of John Canne in the clandestine printing of these tracts, see J. Wilson in *Church History*, 33 (1964), 38-41. The best general accounts of religion and politics are W. Lamont, *Marginal Prynne* (London, 1963) and *Godly Rule* (London, 1969), and G. Yule, *Puritans in Politics* (Sutton Courtenay, 1981). For the development of English separatism, see M. Tolmie, *The Triumph of the Saints* (Cambridge, 1977).

Exeter   Barry Smith

Come out of her my people:

OR

An Answer to the questions of a Gentlewoman (a professour in the Antichristian Church of England) about Hearing the Publicke Ministers: where it is largely discussed and proved to be sinfull and vnlawfull.

ALSO

A Iust Apologie for the way of Totall Separation (Commonly but falsly called Brownisme) That it is the truth of God, though lighly esteemed in the eyes of the blinde world.

With

A Challenge to Dispute with them publickly before King & Counsell: to prove whatsoever I said at the Pillery against them. Viz. That the Calling of them all is Jure Diabolo: *Even from the Divell himselfe.*

By mee JOHN LILBURNE.

Close Prisoner in the Fleete for the Cause of Christ.

IOHN 10. Ver. 27. 5.
My Sheepe heare my voyce.
For they know not the voyce of strangers.

Printed in the yeare of hope,
of ENGLANDS purgation,
& the Prelates dissolution.
ANNO 1639.

The Publisher to the Reader.

COVRTEOVS READER:

IT pleaseth the Lord in this latter age of the world to giue vs sundry helpes, whereby the man of sinne, (with all that bloodie Crew) is more and more discovered: and Gods elect lead (as it were) by the hand out of Babylon.

If any therefore (shutting their eyes against the light) remaine notwithstanding vnder the yoake of Antichrist: they must make account to feele for it, the sorer and heavier wrath of God.

Touching this Treatise what it is, I shall leave it to thy triall and censure, and as thou findest profit by the reading thereof, so blesse God for it, and be ready to communicate the good which thou receivest, vnto the profit of others. Farewell and pray for mee.

      Who is thy truely loving friend
      and Countrie-man.

Alwayes give prayse to God, and let him have the glory of all.

KInd and Loving Chriſtian Freind; I kindly ſalute you in our Lord and Saviour *Ieſus Chriſt*, Beſeeching him, that his enlightning ſpirit, the Spirit of Truth, may both now and ever be with you, and remaine with you, and all thoſe that deſire to ſerve and worſhip God, in all his commandements, according to his revealed will, & not according to mens precepts and devices, which is odious and abominable to him; *Math.* 15 9 *Col.* 2 *Gal.* 4. 9. 10. *Eſay* 66. 3.

But now to give an anſwer to that which you deſire, I ſay, and that in the words of truth, that the thing, as it is to me expreſſed, is very falſe, and therefore I have wrong done me by them that doe report it; and I would deſire you to know of my reſpected Freind the party that told you who they are that did report it.

It ſeemes they ſay, that I have ſaid, that I would as ſoone heare the devill, as Doctor *Stoughton*, or M: *Walker*, which thing is very falſe, for I never ſaid it, nor medled with any particular perſons; But yet thus much I have ſaid, and ſtill doe affirme and maintaine, and will at all times be ready to make it good, and ſeale it with my blood: That the Prelates all of them are Limbs of the Beaſt, ſpoken of *Rev.* 13 2. and alſo, that all thoſe Officers and Miniſters, that are made by them, are all of them Antichriſtian; the beſt as well as the worſt; And we have as good warrant to heare or give eare to the worſt, as well as the beſt; For I proved in my ſpeech, that the beſt of the Miniſters calling is as bad as the worſt of them; for they are all ſent by the Prelates, Chriſts profeſſed and knowne enemies, and they doe preach by vertue of their inſtituting of them, into the Office of Preiſthood, unto whoſe power they ſubmit and take an Oath of Canonicall odedience; And this doe the best among them, (as well as the worst) that take upon them a Parochiall chardge, for they are not sent from Christ, to preach the Gospell, or by vertue of his power, which he hath left in the bodies of his particular (not Nationall) Churches, to choose or ordaine Officers to preach the Word; But by vertue of Antichrists power and authority; from whom they have as really their calling and power given them to preach, as those Officers that were ordained and instituted in the New Testament to preach Christs Gospell, had their power from him; and this ere long you shall see fully proved, though I be never hereafter able to set pen to paper.

Some thing concerning this I said in my speech, as in it you may reade, but it was but a little for the maine thing and strength of my Argument, was behinde, which I could not make knowne, by reason of the Gagg; But I looke and expect to come there againe, or to a worse place; and by the strength and might of my God; I will, come life, come death; speake my minde freely and couragiously; for I am studying to fitt my selfe for it, and I doubt not but by the might of the Lord of Hosts, who is my strength and refuge, to reade them such a Lecture, that shall make the Beast roare, and blaspheme the God of Heaven for madnesse, though I be hewen in peeces when I have done; For I feare neither the Devill, nor his Agents the Prelates, in this cause of my God, and the Lord hath sheltred me under the shadow of his wings, *Psal* 91 under whose protection I am secure and safe from all danger and harme, for though it seaze upon me, yet shall it not overcome me, therefore will I not feare what man can doe unto me, for God is my salvation, I will trust, and not be affrayde, for the Lord *Iehovah* is become my salvation, *Esay.* 12. 2. *Exod.* 15 2.

I have in part, in a briefe way, since I was whipped, declared my minde and judgement to some freinds, because I did feare false reports, and I am alwayes ready, according to the command of the Holy Ghost, to give an answer to every man that shall aske me a reason of the hope that is in me, with meekenesse & feare, 1 *Pet.* 3. 15.

And I now desire to impart a little of my minde unto you, but for my owne part I will perswade no man to beleeve me, nor no man whatsoever, but only to beleeve *Iesus Christ*, speaking in the Scripture, it being the intire and absolute rule of Faith, and that unerring touchstone, that is able to try gold from drosse, neither would I have any to take upon them the profession of that way, the truth of which I am fully convinced off; and am able to any man breathing for my judgement to give a reason, and grounded answer; But for others my advice is to them, as one wishing well to the soules of all my Fellow Brethren and Sisters, Fellow heires of the same Kingdome with me, that they would not take up things lightly and slightly, but labour to gett inward principles in their owne soules.

And

And to get a ground and bottome for their owne spirits, for these things they professe and hold, that so they may not build upon the sand, but upon the unmoveable Rock, the Lord *Iesus Christ*, that shall never be shaken, that so they may, though all the power of darknesse set themselves against them, yet that they may cleave close to God, & our Saviour Christ, and the purity of his Gospell, for we must looke for fanning and sifting, and for the fiery tryall; therefore let us sit downe and reckon, what it will cost us, and if we be not willing to lose all for his sake, yea and to hate all even Father and Mother, riches & life, &c. if they stand in our way to keep us from him, we are not worthy of him *Math.* 10. 37. and 16. 24. *Mark* 8. 34. *Luke* 9. 23. 24. and 14. 26. 27.

And for my owne part, the Lord himselfe hath so firmly by his owne enlightening Spirit so fully convinced me, and setled my soule so unmoveably in his truth, that I assuredly know, that all the power in Earth, yea and the gates of Hell it selfe shall never be able to move me or prevaile against me, for the Lord who is the worker of all my workes in me and for me, hath founded and built me upon that sure & unmoveable foundation the Lord *Iesus Christ*, and I know if ten thousand deaths for my conscience and the cause of my God, (for which with courage and rejoycing I now beare witnesse to, and am close prisoner in bonds, lying day and night in Fetters of Iron, both hands & legges) should be inflicted upon me, I should sing, rejoyce & triumph in them all; For my God makes me glory in my tribulation, and my soule is filled so full of that sweetnesse and joy, that it findes in my God alone that my tongue and penne is never able to the full to expresse & utter it, (to his praise I desire to speake it,) and I doe beleeve, that it is not possible for any man in any condition whatsoever (whose neck in the best doth stoope to the yoake of Antichrist) to have his heart and spirit elevated and lifted up above it selfe in that high degree, with spirituall joy and comfort, divine and heavenly strength and supportation that mine is, for the Holy Ghost saith, they have no rest night nor day who worship the Beast and his Image, and whosoever receiveth the marke of his name; And I doe beleeve it to be true, as I am able to speake by my owne experience; For they may have some spirit of rest and peace, and sudden Flashes of joy and comfort, but when a storme or Tempest doth arise, they are so possessed, with base and cowardly feare and distraction of spirit, that they are like men without hearts, and are ready to runne into every hole, to hide their heads from the face of man, a poore worme, being ready to say (when a tempest ariseth) with them in the 6. *Rev.* 16. 17. Let the Mountaine and Rock fall on us, and hide us from the face of him that sitteth on the Throne, and from the wrath of the Lamb, for the great day of his wrath is come, and who shall be able to stand; When as on the contra-

ry,

ry, the Righteous is as bold as a Lyon, though the wicked fly when none persueth, *Prov.* 28.1. & 18.10. The name of the Lord is a strong Tower, the Righteous runneth unto it and are safe.

And *Psal.* 91. he that dwelleth in the secret place of the most high, shall abide under the shaddow of the Almighty, and he shall be safe from the feare of all danger, as the Holy Ghost there doth declare; So that we see the feare and terrour that possesseth the hearts and spirits of all those whose necks are either in part or in whole under the spirituall yoake and bondage of the Beast; And also the rest and peace, and holy security that they are in that submitt alone to the Lord *Iesus Christ*, for their spirituall Lord and King; And are willing to follow him, wheresoever he goes, not loving their soules to the death, *Rev.* 12. but keepe close and hold fast the name and faith of Christ, even where Satan hath his Throne. *Rev.* 2.13. for he hath said and promised unto his people that keepe close to him, because thou hast kept the word of my patience; I will also keepe thee from the houre of Temptation, which shall come upon all the World, to try them that dwell upon the Earth, *Rev.* 3.10. And this have I found by experience, since the Lord in great mercy and rich loving kindnesse, by his strength and power inabled me to withdraw my soule totally and finally from the greatest spirituall yoake and bondage, that ever any mortall man groaned under, namely the spirituall yoake and bondage of the Beast, or Roman State, unto which, whosoever is hated of the Lord, and doth not belong unto him, doe submitt & yeeld, *Rev.* 9.4. and 12.7,9 & 13.8. But the Lord from all eternity hath loved me with his everlasting love, hath delivered my soule from it, and set me at liberty, and in a large place, and hath given me rest and ease, and hath put a song of prayer and thanksgiving into my mouth, unto the Lord of glory and the Lamb that sitts upon his Throne, who is blessed for ever and ever, and my God hath filled my soule so full of Heavenly matter, that had I but a current vent, I could *ex tempore* write an hundred Sheetes of paper to you, filled full of Heavenly expressions of the Lords goodnesse, faithfulnesse, loving kindnesse and Truth, for my soule is ravished with that fulnesse, sweetnesse, aimeablenesse, and beautifulnesse, that I finde in my God; Oh that my soule were altogether with him, that I might be satisfyed with his fulnesse, and might solace my soule face to face, which I most confidently know I shall in his due time; But, Oh I say againe and againe, that I were with him, for he hath crucifyed the World, and all things here below unto me, and hath enabled me to account and esteeme all things besides himselfe, as dung and durt, not being worthy of casting any affectionate eye upon them, *Philip.* 3. 8.9. and he hath pitched my soule upon himselfe, as a naked and a single object, in whom alone the quintessence of delight, beautie, and satisfaction is to be had, enjoyed, and possessed, and for my shackled

con-

condition that I am in, it is most sweete and pleasant to me, in which I am as merry, yea more chearefull, then ever I was in any condition in my life, and can sleepe as soundly in my Boots and Irons, as *Peter* did betweene the two Souldiers, when he was in prison, who when the Angell of the Lord came to him, to deliver him; He was faine to smite him, before he awaked, *Acts* 12.5.7. And I doe sing *Psalmes*, and I am as merry as *Paul* and *Sylas* were, when they were in the Stocks, and in prison, who sung Psalmes and Prayses at midnight, so that the Prisoners heard them, *Acts* 16.24.25. for the Lord hath so strengthened me with divine power and strength, for the Lord of Hosts is my confidence; And in the Lord *Iehovah* there is everlasting strength; And there is no torments, that the greatest Tyrans in the World can inflict upon me, that can make me miserable, sad, or discontented, for I know all my torments make but way for a greater degree of glory, which I am confident one day I shall be possessour off, and I long with *Paul* to be dissolved and to be with Christ, not out of any trouble or burdensomenesse, that I finde or see in my present afflicted distressed condition, (according to the flesh) but to me it is sweete and joyfull in the Lord, and I know when the Lord hath fully tried me, and done his good pleasure with me, and by me, I shall come out of the Furnace purified and clensed from my drosse filth and corruption, *Iob* 23, for the Lord already in part hath refined me, but not with Silver, for he hath chosen me in the furnace of affliction, *Esay*.48.10.

This by way of *Preface* or *Apology* for my selfe; And now I come to the matter.

And for my owne judgement, it beeing matter concerning the glory and prayse of my God, although I know it will be very unpleasing unto the Pallets of many yea of my neare and deare freinds, from whom I have received expressions of love and kindnesse, whose loving affection, it may be, may be turned to a distast to my person, and my suffering, which if it bee, I shall patiently beare it, for the sincerity of my heart is knowne unto God, who is the searcher of the heart, and the tryer of the reines, *Rev*.2.23.*Ier*.11.20. and 17.10. And I will call him to record, and to beare witnesse, that the glory of his great and holy name, is the single object of all my actions, undertakings, and proceedings; And if I shall incurre hatred therefore from my freinds, I shall comfort my selfe with that which my saviour hath said, which is that he came not to send peace on Earth, but a sword, for I am (saith he) to set a man at variance against his Father, and the daughter against her Mother, and the daughter in Law against her Mother in Law, *Math*.10.34.35. *Luke* 12 49 51.53. and with that which *Paul* comforted himselfe with, if he could approve his heart to God, he did not care what man said of him, for saith he, doe I seeke, to please men,

for

for if J yet please men, I should not be the servant of Christ, *Gal.* 1. 10.

But now for my judgement, for my owne part, if I should never heare a Sermon while I live, yet I should never dare to heare one from any man, good or bad, that is made a Minister by the Prelates, or any of their Creatures, or by vertue of any of their muddy Antichristian Lawes, neither dare I have any spirituall communion with them, so long as they stand in their calling, in regard I am perswaded that he that heareth them sinneth, having no warrant out of the booke of God to doe it, and by undenyable consequence I will prove it, that whosoever heares them so long as they Officiat by vertue of their calling and power, which they have received from the Bishops, to preach, doth heare the Devill; for the Holy Ghost saith, *Rev.* 13 4. the subjects of the Kingdome of the Beast worshipped the Dragon, (that is to say the Devill, which gave power unto the Beast, and they worshipped the Beast, saying, who is like to the Beast, who is able to warre with the Beast.

Now, let us not thinke that they did fall downe to the Devil himselfe, and doe homage to him, face to face, for we never reade of any that did this, but the Holy Ghost doth here declare, that all those that stoope or yeeld in the least to the Lawes of the Beast doth worship & serve the Devill, from whom he hath received his power.

But all the Ministers doe stoope unto his Lawes, which none of them are able to deny, there o e they are as really his servants and subjects, all the time they doe so as they can be.

And we have no ground out of the Scripture to judge better of them;

As they are not the subjects and servants of Christ, that intyrely doe not stoope unto his Lawes and Scepter; For is he, or can he be said to be a subject to the King of England, that stoopes, submitts, & yeelds to the Lawes and Scepter of any other King, his greatest and professedst enemy upon the Earth.

No, without doubt; But they doe stoope to the Lawes of Antichrists Kingdome, who is the greatest and professedst enemy that ever *Iesus Christ* had in the World, as I will be ready to prove to the faces of the best of them in any publick disputation.

Therefore they are really and truely his servants; for his servant you are to whom you obey.

Now, *Iesus Christ* saith to his Disciples, he that heares you, heareth me, and he that heareth me, heareth him that sent me.

So on the contrary, he that heares the Ministers, heares the Prelates that made and sent them; And he that heares the Prelates, heares the Pope, that authorised & gave them their authority; And he that heares the Pope, heares the Devill, that gave him his power; So that I say we
can-

can not partake with them in hearing, or in any administrations of Gods sacred things, but we must of necessity partake of their calling and institution, by vertue of which they officiat and administer; And that I prove from *Pauls* words in the first of the *Cor.* 10. 18. *Are not they which eate of the Sacrifice partakers of the Altar*; Even so I say, are not they which partake of their administration, partakers of their institution? Yea without doubt or question. Now, for their institution, it is not from God (as I will maintaine against them all) therefore we are not to heare them, nor in the least to partake with them or their administration.

And for your better satisfaction seriously reade and weigh the 10. of *Iohn*: And to me it seemes so cleare and plaine, that I doe not doubt but that we are not to heare any Ministers but those that are made by vertue of the Lawes and power of Christ, which he hath left to his Church, in his last will and Testament, which Lawes are unalterable and unchangeable to the end of the World, *Acts* 1.3. 1 *Tim.* 6. 13. 2 *Tim.* 13. 14. 15. 17. *Heb.* 3. 1. 2. 6. *Math.* 28. 19. 20.

But they are not made by vertue of the Lawes and power of Christ, but by the Lawes and Authority of Antichrist, and therefore we are not to heare them, for saith Christ, my Sheepe heare my voice, & I know them, and they follow me, and a stranger they will not follow, but will fly from him, for they know not the voice of strangers; Here you see Christ layes it downe, as a signe and a marke to know his Sheepe by, that they will not heare, nor give eare to false Shepheards.

But so are all the Ministers, for they come not in by the dore, but by a false power and Authority; namely, by the power of the man of sinne, Christs implacable enemy.

Therefore it is not Lawfull for any of Gods people, to heare them; For when the Prelates by vertue of his power, bids them, and Authorize them to preach, they doe preach; And when they command them to hold their peace, they are silent, and let their flock runne at randome; whenas a good and true Shepheard layeth downe his life for his Sheepheard.

Object. But many object and say, it is true, that their calling as it comes from the Prelates, is unlawfull, but they have an inward calling, for they are fitted for the worke of the Ministerie.

Answ. To which I answer and say, I reade of no inward calling, that any of those Officers had, that Christ or his Apostles did institute in the New Testament, for the Apostles had their calling from Christ, and the other Officers had their calling from the Churches, where they themselves were members, and over which, by the Lawes and power of Christ, they were made Officers.

But if the Ministers of Antichrist have an inward calling, I desire to see it proved by the Scripture; And as for their qualifications and fit-

B   enesse

nesse for the Ministrie. I deny, and say, that they are not qualified according to the command of Christ, by *Paul* to *Timothy* & *Titus*; And I doe affirme and will maintaine it, that no man ought to be Elected for the worke of the Ministrie, unlesse he have all those qualifications that is by the Holy Ghost set downe in the 1 *Tim.* 3. and the first of *Titus.*

Now, there is none of them, yea the best among them, that hath the qualification for a Bishop, a Pastor, or an Elder, which is all. One must not be a Novice, least being lifted up with pride, he fall into the condemnation of the Devill. Also he must hold fast the faithfull word as it hath been taught, that he may be able by sound Doctrine, both to exhort and convince the gainesayers; But none of them have either of these, for they are so farre from being able to convince gainesayers by sound Doctrine, that they are but novices in many things, and either wilfully or ignorantly are blinde of the naked wayes of God, being darkned with the smoake which came out of the bottomlesse pitt, *Rev.* 8. 2, and I will justify it to the faces of the best of them, that they are enemies to the Kingly Office of *Iesus Christ*, and the right government of his Church, both in practise and in judgement; and therefore are not fit (take them at the best) to be Pastors over Christs Sheepe; Neither can any of them say as *Paul* did, *Acts* 20. That he was cleare of the blood of all men, in that he ceased not to declare unto them, the whole Counsell of God, which every faithfull Pastor ought to doe; but none of them have done it, nor are able, for as I said before, they are ignorant of it, and are enemies to it, as they doe witnesse in their Pulpits, where they preach against the naked and pure wayes of God, and the Professours of it, but none of them dare to enter the list of a Publick set dispute.

Object. I but say others they preach the Word of God, and that cannot be corrupted by their calling, but remaine the Word of God still, therefore we may Lawfully heare it from them.

Answ. I answer, they preach the outside of the Word, it is true, but the marrow and pith of it, they meddle but little with, for the best of them are yet ignorant of the marrow, of many choice Truths of God, for their understandings are so overspred with the Foggie Mists of the darke and black Kingdome of *Antichrist*, that they want spirituall eyes to see it; And behold it untill the Lord in mercy if so he please to open their eyes; And what though they doe preach the Word, they have no authority from God so to doe, if they have, let them stand up and show it, and prove it; Not with human learning, but by the authority of the Scripture.

It is true, the Devill himselfe preached Christ, and made a glorious confession of him, saying: *I know that thou art Iesus the Christ, the Son of God, Mark* 1 24.

This

This if it had come from one of Christs owne servants, it had been most acceptable, and well pleasing to him, but in regard it comes from the Devill, he will not owne it, but commands him to hold his peace.

It is very true, the Word of God is good and sweete, and a comfort to the soules of his servants, if it be preached by any that hath authority from Christ, we are bound to heare it; But the best of the Ministers have no authority or warrant from Christ to preach the Word, nor we to heare it from them, *Ioh. 10.2.3.5. Hos. 9.4. Psal. 50.16.*

But to the wicked saith God, *What hast thou to doe to declare my Statutes, or that thou shouldest take my Covenant in thy mouth.*

Now looke upon all of them to be such as God here speakes off, in regard of their institution and standing, being visible members of Antichrists Kingdome; I doe not, nor will not meddle with their persons, nor no mans else, but only with their sinfull and wicked station and standing; Which as I am a subject to Christs Kingdome, and a prisoner in bonds and fetters of Iron, for his cause, I am bound in conscience so to doe it, *Iudg. 5.23. Curse ye Meroz* (saith the Angell of the Lord) *yea curse ye bitterly the inhabitants therein, because they came not forth, to the helpe of the Lord against the mighty.* Yea the Spirit of God saith; That they are blessed and happy that takes Babels Bratts, and dash them against the stones, *Psal. 137.8.9.*

But they are all Sonnes and Children of Spirituall Babell or Babylon, *Rev. 11.8.* and *14.8.* and *18.2.*

Now, by vertue of their being members of his Kingdome, we have no ground or warrant out of the Word of God, to heare them, for it is impossible to be a servant and a subject both to Christ and Antichrist; But they are subjects to Antichrists Kingdome; Therefore cannot be said truely to be subjects and servants to Christ.

For is not he properly a subject to the King of *Spains*, that submits to his Lawes, and beares Office under him, by vertue of his authoritie; And can such men, while they doe so, be said and truely to be esteemed to be subjects to the King of England, unto whose Lawes they doe not submit; Without doubt they cannot. Even so can the Ministers or Preists (for so is their institution) who submit unto the Lawes of Antichrist, and beare Office under him, and execute their Office by vertue of his power and Authoritie, and therefore are his Servants and Subjects, and cannot truely be said to be the Servants and Subjects of Christ, unto whose Lawes they doe not submit.

Therefore we are not to heare them, or to have any thing to doe with them, *Rev. 18.4. 2 Cor. 6.17.*

B 2　　　　　　　　　　　　　　　　Againe

Againe, *Mount Sion*, that is to say, the Church of God is the place which God hath chosen, and hath promised his presence and blessing, *Psal.*132.13.14.15.and 83.17. 2 *Cor.*6.16. Now, I would know where any of his people hath any warrant to seeke his presence and blessing any where but where he hath promised it; But he never promised it in the visible Assemblies of Antichrists Kingdome; Therefore we have no ground or warrant to seeke it there, or come there at all; Much more concerning this I have and am able to say but I am above measure straightned, for want of a fitting opportunitie; and there fore for your further satisfaction, repaire to the perusall of a little thing, called a declaration, where the people of God are to seeke his presence and blessing, only in *Mount Sion*, the Citty and Church of God, *Psal.*46.4.and 48.1.2.8. *Esay*.60.14. and 62.11.12. and not in the Assemblies of Antichrist, being Cages of uncleane Birds, *Rev.*18.2. *Esay.*13.21.22.

Againe, I see no ground or warrant, that any of Gods people have, to have any spirituall communion with them, in regard God hath commanded his people, at all times, very strictly, that they shall have no communion with Idolaters, nor their Idols, as the whole Booke of God doth declare; and I desire you to read the *seventh of Deut:* and there you shall see Gods strict command to that end. But the Ministers all of them are Idolaters, yea Idols themselves; Therefore we must have no communion with them. Now, that they are Idolaters, is as cleare as the Sun, that shines at noone-day; And that they are Idols, I am able to prove it to their faces; For an Idoll is nothing else according to the Scripture but a Creature or Creatures set a part, or instituted to worship God with or by, which he himselfe never ordained for that end and purpose; But such are all the prelates Ministers, for they were never of his ordaining or instituting, but of his greatest enemies, the Pillars of Antichrists Kingdome, by vertue of whose power they officiate; Therefore they are Idols, whom all Gods people, that are faithfull Souldiers and leige Subjects, ought to be a meanes, and a helpe, to roote up and pull downe.

Now, this definition of an Idoll is not only according to the Scripture, but is given by the soundest Nonconformists themselves, as you may read in their Bookes, where they have strongly proved the Surplice, and the Crosse in *Baptisme*, and kneeling in the Act of receiving the Communion; And the rest of the Prelates instituted sacred Ceremonies, as they call them, saying in their Reasons before the Common-prayer, for the retaining of some Ceremonies, and the abolishing of others, that they are apt to stirr up the dull minde of man, to the remembrance of some duty to God, by some speciall signification, whereby he might be edifyed.

Now

Now, if you reade the *Scots Dispute*, which was printed at *Leyden*, in Holland, the last Summer, you shall there find strong reasons, to prove the Ceremonies Idols; and his maine Argument is, because they are not of Gods institution, but of sinfull mans ordaining.

Also that Noble and worthy Doctor (whom I so much honour and respect) Doctor *Bastwicke*, in his Booke, called *The Vanity and Impiety of the old Lettany*, doth prove it to be an Idoll, yea and calls it a damnable soule-murthering Idoll; And that upon the same ground, because it is not of Gods, but of mans institution, without any ground or warrant from God; and therefore is an Idoll, and is to be detested as an abominable Idoll. Now, what they say of the Ceremonies, and of the Service, the same I say of the Prelates, and all the Ministers that are made by them, and have their calling from the Bishops, they are Creatures set apart to worship God with or by, but were never of his instituting, or by vertue of his power, but by mans institution, and by vertue of the power of the greatest enemy that ever *Iesus Christ* had, or his Kingdome ever had on Earth, namely *Antichrist*, or the Kingdome of the Beast, *Rev* 9.3.7.10.11. and 13.6.7.16.17. and 12.6.7.15.17.

And therefore they are Idols, whom so long as they stand in their places and callings under the spirituall Antichristian authority, which they all submit to and subject themselves to, I shall not dare to have any spirituall communion with them, either in publicke or private, for what fellowship hath righteousnesse with unrighteousnesse; Or what communion hath light with darknesse; And what Concord hath Christ with *Beliall*? Or what part hath he that beleeveth with an Infidell? Or what agreement hath the Temple of God with Idols? Surely, none at all. Wherefore come you out from among them, and be you seperate, saith the Lord, and touch no uncleane thing, and I will receive you, and will be a Father unto you, and you shall be my Sonnes and Daughters, saith the Lord Almighty, 2 *Cor*.6.14. to the end. *Esay.* 52.11. *Ier.* 51.6.7. *Rev.* 18.4.5.

Besides this, tnough I am, and doe respect them as men, being the Creatures of God, and doe reverence them as they are privy Counsellours, and Head-members of the State; though it be not sutable in the least to their false pretended spirituall calling. But as they are Bishops and Officers in the Kingdome of the Beast, my knee and submission and reverence, shall by the strength of my God, be as litle to them, as *Mordecay* was to proud *Haman*, who was King *Ahashuerosh*, Cheife Favorite, being above all the Princes that were with him, *Hest.* 3.1. Yet *Mordecay* would not so much as bow to him, or doe him any reverence, *verse the* 3. though it doe procure me as much wrath from the, as it did *Mordecay* from *Haman*, of whom the Holy Gost saith, he was full of wrath, seeing *Mordecay* would not reverence him, *Vers.* 5.6.

Neither will I ever give baile to them, or part with any money, either to them or any of their Creatures, for any thing whatsoever, unlesse it be meerely for Temporall and Earthly things, in regard I doe beleeve it is the duty of all Gods people, who desire to glorify him in their lives and conversations, and to shine as so many burning Lamps in the midst of a perverse and crooked generation, as they ought and should doe; Neither to bow finger, knee, or hatt unto any of them, or to doe them any reverence, as they are Bishops and Cheife Pillars in the Kingdome of Antichrist, for by vertue of their calling and Office, they are the deadly and implacable enemies of God, and are so many pernicious and damnable Idols (by which God is exceedingly dishonoured) set up by the Devill in the Kingdome of the Beast, *Rev.* 9. 3. and 13. 2. 4. and 16. 13. 14. And I can prove it, that it was as Lawfull for the 3 Children, to worship or bow to *Nebuchadnezars* Idoll, as for Gods people to bow and doe homage to them.

And for my owne part, if they require of me any such, my answer shall be to them, as the 3 Children was to the King. *Dan* 3. 16. 17. 18. Be it knowne to you Bishops and Doctors, I feare you not; or the God whom I serve and feare, is able to deliver me out of your hands, and from your Tyrannising crueltie; But if he doe not, be it knowne unto you, Oh ye Prelates, that I will not serve you, nor worship you, nor yeeld nor submit in any spirituall things unto you; And if I were at liberty, I would professe those Truths of God surely without feare, which he himselfe hath made knowne unto me; And if I were at any time taken by any of their Officers, I would not goe to prison with them, unlesse they carried me by force; Yet if it were the meanest Officer in the Kingdome that tooke me, that were made an Officer by vertue of the Kings Authority and power, I would submit unto him, and goe with him, whether he would have me, for I know the Kings Authority is from God; And if I should disobey it, I should disobey God, and sinne against God, and breake his Command, *Rom.* 13. And therefore I will obey him, his Lawes, and all those that beare his Authority, in all things they command or enjoyne me; without any the least resistance at all, heartily from my heart, either actively or passively; for if they command me any thing that is not contrary to the Word of God, I will obey them actively; But if they command me any thing that is dishonourable to God or his Truth, I dare not in the least obey them actively, but say with the Apostle, whether it be fitt to obey God or Men, judge ye, for we ought to obey God rather then Men, *Acts* 5. 29. Yet I will submit my body to them, and suffer cheerfully, without any grudging any thing they shall inflict upon me, for I doe hold it unlawfull for any of Gods people, in their greatest Oppression by the Majestrate, to rebell or to take up any Temporal armes against them, whether the Oppression be in Spirituall or Temporall things,

but

but only to pray and make use of Gods two edged Sword, *Heb.4.12.* *Rev.19.15.* and waite upon with patience for redresse and deliverance, and to seeke unto him for strength, that they may willingly and couragiously suffer any Terrours or Torments that they will inflict upon them, for standing close to God, and his naked Truth and cause.

But to the Kingdome of the Beast, these members of which the Prelates are, will I never stoope by the might of the Lord of Hosts, nor have any spirituall communion with them, for the Lord hath expresly commanded me and all his people to have nothing to doe with Idols, nor with Idolaters, *1 Cor.10.14. 1 Iohn 5.21. Exod.23.32. Deut.7.1.2.3.4.5.* and *12.3.* Now, they are the greatest Idolaters that ever were in the world, and the most pernitious Idols, that are upon the Earth. *Rev:9.20.* & cap:17.for they haue a golden Cup put in their hands, it is full of abomination & filthines, & with it they dazle the eyes of the world, & make it to cōmit close & hidde fornication, & Idolatrie, which is the greatest and most dangerous Idolatrie that is, for they couer their wickednesse and deceiveablenesse over with the Name of the Lamb, but for all that doe the deeds of the Dragon. *Rev.13.11. Iohn 8.44.* But if they professed Idolatry openly to the eyes of the World, the people would detest them, but they doe it closely and covertly, and therefore are not so easily discerned, but deceive very many, *Math. 24. 5.* And therefore the Beasts Kingdome is called, as it is indeed, the Misterie of iniquitie, *2 Thess 2.7.*

Now, I will maintaine it, that the Kingdome of the Beast is the greatest Idol that ever was in the World, and the greatest plague that ever God sent into the World, as the *Revelation of Saint Iohn* doth declare, and as appeares by the expressions of the Spirit of God, in the 8. Chapter, where we may read, that when the 4. First Angels had sounded their Trumpets, mighty and horrible plagues then followed them, worse and more great were to come after, as appeares by the vehement expressions and calling out of the Holy Ghost, with a loud voice, *Verse the last ;* Saying, *Woe, Woe, Woe to the inhabitants of the Earth* (reitterating 3 times together) *by reason of the other voices of the Trumpet of the three Angels which are yet to sound.* For why the fifth Angell in the first Verse of the next Chapter sounded, then followed a mighty & horrible plague to all the inhabitants of the world; The like whereof was never heard off before, and that is the smoake that came out of the bottomlesse pitt, which was that horrible darkenesse, and spirituall blindnesse and sottish ignorance that seazed upon the World, dureing the time of the Beasts Kingdome; which was so great, that the visible face of a Church of Christ could not be found upon the Earth, for the heavens departed as a scroll together, *Rev.6.14.*

And

And out of this smoake or darknesse came the Locufts the beafts officers or Clergy, which are a multitude in number, there being in the Kingdome of *Antichrift* at this day above an hundred feverall Officers; Whereas in the Kingdome of Chrift there is but 5. Namely, Paftor, Teacher, Elder, Deacon, and Widdow, *Rom.* 12.7.8. *Ephef.* 4.11. *Phil.* 1.1. 1 *Tim.* 3.1.2. and 5. *Titus* 1.5.7.

Againe, the Spirit of God pronounceth another woe to the inhabitants of the Earth and of the Sea, for the Devill is turned downe unto you, having great wrath, becaufe he knoweth that he hath but a fhort time, the like expreffion we read not of in the whole Booke of God, nor that there were any fuch plagues fince the beginning of the World; As thofe were which came along with the Kingdome of the Roman Beaft, as the Stories of all ages, fince his beginning, is able to witneffe and prove, for men worfhipped the Devill, and committed fuch horrible wickedneffe, for which God fent fuch mighty plagues upon them, as the like before was never heard of before in the world, as the whole *Booke of the Revelation* doth witneffe; Therefore of all Idols that ever were in the World, Gods people have moft caufe of all to deteft, abhorre, and abominate the Idolaters and the Idols in the Kingdom of the Beaft, & whofoever the Lord loves he will deliver fro them; *Rev.* 20.4. But thofe that are his enemies, and hated of him, fhall continue in fubjection to it, *Rev.* 9.4 and 13.8. and 14.9.10.11. and 19.20. *Pro.* 2.18.19. and 5.5. and 7.27. and 9.18.

Now, the time of the raigne and durance of the Kingdome of the Beaft, in the 11. *Rev.* 2. is faid to be 42 moneths; and in the 12. *Rev.* 14. it is called a time times and halfe a time, which is three yeares and a halfe; And in the firft Verfe of this Chapter, it is tearmed to be 1260 dayes, which is juft 42 moneths, reckoning 30 dayes to every moneth, and it makes alfo three yeares and a halfe, accounting 12 Moneths to every yeare; and this is the time of the Raigne of the Beaft, or the durance of Antichrifts Kingdome; Which if we reckon each day for a yeare, as the Lord himfelfe in Scripture doth, as we may read when the Spies that went from the Tents of Ifraell, at the Lords command, to fearch the Land of *Canaan*, which they were a doing 40 dayes; And at their returne they gave out an evill report of it, which made the people to finne and rebell againft God, and not to give credit to his word, Oath and promife, which was to bring them into the Land of *Canaan*, to give it to them, notwithftanding the greatneffe and potency of the Heathen, for the Lord himfelfe had promifed to caft them out, but becaufe they beleeved him not, but rebelled againft him, fearing the ftrength and power of the Heathen, the Lord would make them to wander in the barren and defart Wilderneffe 40 yeares. For faith he, after the number of the dayes, in which ye fearched the Land even 40 dayes, each day for a yeare, fhall you beare your iniquities, even 40 yeares, and you shall know my breach of promise, *Numb*. 14. 34. *Ezek*: 4. 5. 6. where God saith thus to the Prophet : I have laid upon thee the yeares of iniquity, according to the number of the dayes, three hundred and ninety dayes, so shalt thou beare the iniquity of the House of Israel ; and when thou hast accomplished them, lye againe on thy right side, and thou shalt beare the iniquity of the house of *Iudah* 40 dayes, I have appointed each day for a yeare. So that if we expound the 1260. by these 2 places of scripture, reckning as God himselfe doth each day for a yeare; which I verily beleeve is the right meaning of the Holy Ghost; We shall finde that the Beasts Kingdome shall endure from the beginning to the end 1260. yeares; For I see no ground that these places should be expounded litterally for three yeares and a halfe, and no more, for it is impossible that Antichrist should doe all these strange things, in so short a time, that is said, he shall doe & fulfill, therefore without doubt it must be expounded each day for a yeare, for the man of sinne was a working in the Apostles time, but the Emperour who letted him, kept him out of his seate till he was taken away, 2 *Thes*. 2. 7. Now, during the time of Antichrist, the Holy Cittie, or the true Church of God, is to be troden under foote, *Rev*. 11. 2. and to be in a sad and afflicted condition, and to be persecuted by the beast, and the members of his state & Kingdome all that time, *Rev*. 13 7. 15. and Chapt. 12. though now and then she should have some breathing and refreshing times; And when Antichrists Kingdome growes to an end, (which blessed be God doth hasten apace,) the Foggie Mists of darkenesse, blindnesse and ignorance, which is *the smoake* that the Holy Ghost saith, *came out of the bottomlesse pitt*; *Rev*. 9. shall in some measure be dispeld, and the Beames of Truth and spirituall light, shall breake and shine out, as is plaine in the 10. 14, and 16. Chapters; for then the Booke of Life the Holy Scripture is opened, which in former ages lay altogether hid, and in a manner shutt up in obscurity & darknesse, as appeares plainly out of the 11. Chapt. Therefore let us not wonder, nor think it strange that the eyes of spirituall understanding, (which is to know, see & imbrace the naked Truths of God,) is opened of so few of the great and famous men, in the eye of the World, but continue still enemies to the bare & naked Truths of God, for the Kingdome of the Beast is not yet destroyed, & the smoake of the bottomlesse pitt hath so darkened the Sunne & the aire, that the spirituall eyes of few mens understandings, are opened to see & take notice of the intyre Truths of God; yet notwithstanding let us take heede, that we be not offended & stumble to our destruction ; *Luke* 20, 17 18. 1 *Pet*. 2. 8. at the naked wayes and cleare and pure Truth of Christ, because they are but few and meane in the estimation of the World, that doth imbrace them, and professe them, for the Church of *Smirna*, though shee were but poore and meane in the eye of the World, yet shee was rich in Gods account, becaufe fhe kept clofe to his naked wayes and Truths, *Rev*.2 9.whereas on the contrary *proud and haughty Laodicea*, who was full of outward riches and treafures; And wanted nothing that might make her glitter & fhine in the eyes of the world, yet notwithftanding is odious in the fight of God, becaufe fhe was *luke warme* and neither *hot* nor *cold*, for he threatens to *fpew her out of his mouth*; doe you your felfe make the application; Likewife let us take notice of that thankfgiving, which Chrift gives to his Father: I thanke thee oh Father, Lord of Heaven and Earth, becaufe thou haft hidd thefe things from the wife and prudent, and haft revealed them to Babes, even fo Father, for fo it feemed good in thy fight, *Math*.11.25.26.

The naked purity and Truth of the Gofpell of Chrift, is too homely a thing, for the great learned Doctors of the world, to imbrace, ftoope and fubmitt unto; for Chrift hath faid, that the profeffors of it fhall be hated of all men, yea of their parents, kindred, and Freinds, *Luke* 21. 16.17. *Marke* 13.12. and are accounted as Sheepe to the flaughter, all the day, 1 *Cor*.4. whofe condition is to be afflicted and perfecuted here by the men of the world, *Iohn* 15.18.19. and 16.2.3.33. *Heb*. 12.4.6.7.8. for there muft and will be to the end of the World enmity betweene the feede of the woman and the feede of the Serpent, *Gen*.3.15. and therefore falfe Teachers and feducers, though they come in the name of Chrift, and preach part of his Gofpell, *Math*.7. 5; and 24.5. yet they are enemies to Chrift, the purity of his Truth and people, though they make a flowrifhing fhow in the flefh, yet becaufe they love not the Croffe of Chrift, which alwaies goes alonge, and is infeperable from the zealous and ftrict profeffion of him and his Truth, *Prov*.3.11.12. *Heb*.11. *Rev*.3.19, nor will they part with their eafe pleafure and fatt morfels, *Efay*.65.10,11,12, nor *fuffer perfecution with the people of God*, for the Truth of God, as Mofes did, *Heb*:11:25. Therefore they will neither imbrace the purity of the Truth, nor willingly let thofe that would, *Gal*:6:12. Yet for all that though they will not, yet all thofe that defire to approve their hearts and fpirits unto God, and to glorifie him both in their lives & deaths, muft not forfake his Truth, for feare of perfecution, or lofing of their kindred, or Freinds, *Gal*:5:11: *Math*:10:33: *Marke* 8:34:38: *Luke* 14: 26: for here Chrift himfelfe faith, that he that loveth Father or Mother, or his owne life, or any thing elfe more then him, fhall never poffeffe nor enjoy him, neither here nor hereafter; For he faith: He that denies him or his Truth before men, him will he denie before his Father which is in Heaven. Therefore in regard the Gofpell of Chrift, in the ftrict profeffion of it, is fo meane, contemptible and burdenfome a thing in the blinde and darke eyes of the World, and lyes under the reproach and ignominy of the men thereof, the great

Rab-

Rabbies doe stumble at it, and doe not imbrace it, 1 Cor: 1.19.20: for it is written saith God, *I will destroy the wisdome of the wise, and wil bring to nought the vnderstandings of the prudent, where is the wise, where is the scribe, where is the disputer of this world : hath not God made foolish the wisdome of this world Isa:29.14. & 33,18. Oba: verse 8.* Therefore in regard the great Doctors of the world doe not imbrace the wayes of God: the multitude stumble at them, likewise, being ready to say with them *Io: 7, haue any of the Rulers or of the Pharises beleeued on him, but this people who knoweth not the law & are accursed.* Even so say men in these daies, of the naked truths and waies of God: do any of the Rulers or Nobles, or do the great & learned Doctors & famous Divines : imbrace and practice these strict and rugged waies, but onely a companie of *Brownists*, who are the base and obscure fellowes of the world, and a companie of foolish singuler people, contemning and censuring all besides themselues, as though none should be saued but they onely.

To you : Oh yee spirituall blind people, whose vnderstandings are darkned with the smoake of the bottomlesse pitt, and whose braines are intoxicated and drunke with the glittering and gilded Cup of spirituall fornication & abhomination, of the *scarlet whore Reuel·17.*

To you I answere, and know you that the way to heaven is narrow and straite, and Christs fold and flocke, but a small & little company in comparison of the world, *Math: 7. 14. Luke 13.24.* Also know that God hath not called many wise men after the flesh, nor many mighty, nor many noble, but God hath chosen the foolish things of this world, to confound the wise, and God hath chosen the weake things of this World, to confound the things that are mighty; and the base things of the World, and things which are despised, hath God chosen, yea and things which are not, to bring to naught things that are; And he himselfe gives the reason of it, *that no flesh should glory in his presence,* 1 *Cor.* 1.26 27 28. 29. And *Iames* tells us, that God hath chosen the poore of this World, rich in faith, and heires of the Kingdome, which he hath promised to them that love him, *Iames* 2 5.

And what though the Rabbies and great Doctors be learned, yet it is but Earthly and humane learning, which *Paul* had before his conversion, for he was a Pharise brought up at the feete of *Gamaliel*, a great learned Doctor of the Law had in reputation among all the people: *Acts* 5.34, and 22.3. But yet when he came to the true spirituall knowledge of true spirituall learning indeed, which is taught to all Christs Schollers, lesse or more, that are brought up in his Schoole, he renounced his humane Schollership, and accounted it no better then dung or dirt. *Phil:* 3.5.7 8.

But besides him, we read of none of the Apostles, that were learned in that learning, which the blinde world accounts learning and Schol-

C 2 lership

lership, for they were all or most of them poore men, brought up in obscure and base callings many of them being no better then poore Fishermen; yet when Christ called them, he indued them with spirituall learning, which is the true learning indeed ; *Acts* 2. 1. &c.

And those in the new *Testament*, that are commended for their learning, it was because they were filled with the gifts of the Spirit, and were mighty in the Scriptures, *Iohn* 7. 38. 39. *Acts* 18. 24. 1 *Cor.* 12. 3. 7. 8. 10. and 14.

By all which places of Scripture we see, that the learning which made the Apostles famous, was not human learning, (for none of them had it but *Paul*, and he renounced it,) but it was heavenly learning, which came from God, being the gift of his Holy Spirit. And for all the rest of those which they ordained (by the power and Authority which they had from Christ) to officiat in the Churches, and to administer the sacred and holy things of God, to his chosen and sanctifyed ones, (for none but them have true right to Christs ordinances,) it was spirituall knowledge, divine learning, and insight into the Scripture, which are the gifts of the spirit of God, as is before proved; which made them fitt for those Offices, that they were chosen to by the Church, and ordained by the Apostles, for they were not to be *Novices* in the Mysteries and wayes of God, but *found in the Faith*, and also of a holy and Godly life and conversation, which the Apostle calls *a good report*, and to have the rest of those qualifications, which he layes downe in 1 *Tim.* 3. *and* 5. *Chapters*, and *Titus* 1. And whosoever have not these qualifications, are not fitt (according to the Apostles command there) to beare Office in the true Church, which is the spirituall *Sion, Citty, & House of God*; *Psal.* 87 2. 3. and 132. 13. 16. *Esay.* 33. 20. 21. and 52. 1. *Heb.* 12. 22. *Rev.* 20. 9, and 12. 2.

Now, that Heavenly learning, and gifts of the spirit, which the Lord under the time of the Gospell, doth bestow upon his chosen and holy ones, doth fulfill the Prophesies of the Prophets in old time, who Prophesied of the same things, *Esay.* 44 3. 4, and 54. 13; *Ier.* 31; *Ioel* 2. 28; saying : And it shall come to passe afterward, that I will poure out my spirit upon all flesh, and your sonnes and your daughters shall prophesie, your old men shall dreame dreames, and your young men shall see visions, and also upon the hand-maide in those dayes will I poure out my spirit.

Oh! the simplicity, sweetenesse and pleasantnesse of the wayes of God, if we had but inlightened spirituall understandings, to see, behold and looke into them, which if we had, they would ravish our soules, rejoyce our spirits, and fill our hearts full of gladnesse ; But they are sealed and will be hid from us, till the Lord in his rich mercy & loving kindnesse, be pleased to anoynt our eyes with spirituall *Eye-salve*, and take away these Foggie Mists of darknesse & scales of ignorance that

hang

hang upon our understandings; 1 *Cor.* 2. Oh! that the Lord would be pleased to deale so gratiously with us, that we might be fooles & Idiots, emptie & vile in our own eyes, that so we might nakedly lye at the footstoole of Iesus Christ, and seeke for wisedome & spirituall understanding, from him, & him alone, according as it is our duty & the the command of wisedome; *Prov.* 1.4.8, and 9. Chapters. But alas, alas, we have haughty hearts & proud spirits of our owne, and seeke to be something in our selves, and doe not labour to be weaned from all things, in our selves, as is our duty; for we should nakedly goe out of our selves, and this we shall know to be true if ever the Lord come truely and thoroughly to instruct and teach us in his spirituall, heavenly wisedome; It is the greife of my soule, to see people take such paines, *for that which will not profitt; And to lay out their silver for that which is not worth the buying;* Esay. 55. 2. Beeing very zealous in professing the seeming way of God, and yet are full of ignorance & blindnesse, in the true wayes of God, wanting that true spirituall sanctifyed knowledge, and cleare insight into the Scripture, which is taught by the spirit of God, that being true of them, which is said in *Esay.* 59. *That they grope for the wall like blinde men; yea and grope as if they had no eyes, stumbling at noone-day,* as in the night, being in desolate places, as dead men, not knowing that a deceived heart hath turned them aside; being not able to say, that there is a lye in their right hand, as the Prophet in another place speakes: But unto all such in the words of the spirit of God, I say, behold all you that kindle a fire, that compasse your selves about with sparkes, walke in the light of your fire, and in the sparkes that you have kindled; But saith God, this shall you have of my hands; Ye shall lye downe in sorrow, *Esay:* 50. 10.

Because that it is a shame even in the eyes of the World, for a man to be of no Religion; Therfore people take upon them the outward forme of Religion, but are destitute of the inward power of godlinesse, going on in a formall way of Religion, with muddy, earthie, and unsanctified affections, but doe not strive, studdy & labour, as they ought to get inward principles, & true grounds in their owne soules, that so they may be built upon that sure & unmooveable foundation, that never can be shaken; But build upon *sand, hay and stubble*; as the Apostle speakes; And therfore that building will come to ruine, when stormes & Tempests doth arise, as too true experience, hath, doth & will manifest & declare, for when men are not soundly setled in the true wayes they cañot possible have that true inward peace, which God hath promised to his faithfull ones; But their spirits & hearts are full of feares & distractions, in time of danger and calamity, I appeale even to the hearts and spirits, even of people themselves that are not as yet convinced and settled in the right and true wayes of God.

Sure

Sure I am, I am able to speake it by my selfe, and doe speake it in the presence of my God, who knowes my heart, and trieth my reines, *Rev:2.23.* that I have found it true, by former experience; for the Spirit of God saith, *there is no peace to the wicked, Esay.48.22,* and *57. 21.* Now, while a man is out of the true wayes of God, and is in the by-wayes of sinne and wickednesse, he cannot truely according to the revealed will of God, be tearmed any otherwise, then a wicked man; Though notwithstanding his soule may be pretious to God; But we are not to judge according to the secret will, but only to judge according to the revealed will of God, for secret and hidden things belong to God, but revealed things to us and to our children, as *Moses* saith.

But all those that are members of the Kingdome of Antichrist, (as all that submit to the Prelates and their Lawes are) are out of the true wayes and pathes of God, and are in the bye and crooked way of sin and wickednesse; And therefore we have no grounded warrant out of the Scripture, the revealed will of God, to judge or esteeme of them any otherwise but as wicked men, who in that estate cannot be possessours of that true and setled peace and spirituall comfort and joy, that God doth bestow vpon his faith sevants.

Now as for the proofe of this argument, tis every branch & part of it proved in the foregoing discourse; but on the contrary I can truelie speake it, that my soule had never before, that true rest, quietnesse, and sweete inward spirituall peace: that I haue been and am still possessour of, since my God gaue me strength, might & power, to shake of that Antichristian yoake, and all communion with his lawes & subjects. And my soule is filled so full of true rest and peace, that all my torments and sufferings, and the greatnesse and potency of my adversaries, the chiefe of which is the Divell the prince of this world, (working in and by his sonne the P*relate* of *Canterbury*) doth not in the least terrifie or trouble mee, but I am merry and cheerefull in the midst of the veriety of my sufferings, for the Lord makes me to triumph over them all, and I know and beleeue: that if all the Divels in hell, and all his Limbs vpon the earth: do bend themselves against me to overthrow me, yet they shall never make me sadd, for the Lord hath given me a cheerfull and merry heart, which whosoever hath, *Salomon* saith, *hath a continuall Feast, Prov:15.15,* nor make me feare or be affrayde of them, for God is my salvation, I will trust add not be affrayde of them, for God is my salvation, the Lord *Iehovah* is my strength, and my song, he also is become my salvation, *Esay.12.12.* And though the youths doe fainte and be weary, and the younge men utterly faile, yet they that waite upon the Lord, shall renew their strength, they shall mount up with wings as eagles, they shall runne and not be weary, and they shall walke & not be faint, *Esay.40.30.31.* For the Lord is a

strength

strength to the poore, a strength to the needy in his distresse, a refuge from the storme, a shadow from the heate, when the blast of the terrible one is as a storme againft the Wall, *Esay.* 25.4. and the spirit of God saith: that he will keep him in perfect peace whose minde is staied on him, therefore in the Lord will I trust for ever. For in the Lord Iehovah is everlasting strength *Esa:* 26.3.4. and the Lord saith, he keeps his Church and will water it every moment least any hurt it, yea I will keep it night and day saith he. Now I am a true member of it, and therefore haue right and share of the benifitt of this promise, and assuredly knowe that the Lord will so keep me (though I be in the midst of the fire) that mine enemies shall not prevaile nor hurt mee, & though all men forsake me, yet hee will take care of me and provide for me: the young lions shall want & suffer hunger, but they that loue and feare the Lord, shall want no good thing.

But my loving friend, am I become your enemy (because in publicke) I haue spoken the truth, let not your anger and displeasure be further incensed against me, when you haue read this that is here written; I hope you would not haue me, who haue begun in the spirit, to be made perfect in the flesh; Oh God forbid that ever I should so much as entetaine the least thought of that, and therefore know that this is my setled resolution, which the Lord hath wrought in my heart. And for this I will spend and be spent, and be puld in ten thousand peices: before I will in the least deny my God, and his naked truth, or the least tittle of that which he himself by his holy spirit hath made known vnto me **1** *Cor:* 2.10.11.14. And further knowe that all my kindred according to the flesh, hath deserted and forsaken me, in my present condition. But if all my friends (yea and Christian Brethren also) in the the world, should be offended with me, for sticking close to my good cause, and if they should all forsake me and leaue me naked to the world, yea though I starue & rott in Prison, (as I know I shall not) for as long as there was a peice of bread in the bakers street, *Ieremiah* wanted not in his distresses, and I know *Ieremiahs* God is my God, & wil do the like for me as he did for him, if need require. But if I should be like to starue in Prison, yet wil I never in the least, by the strengh & might of my God, feare my enemies, or loue my friends so much as to deny the least of his truths, for their threatnings or cruelty, or for their faunings, flattering, and deceiueable perswasions, for I know if my friends do leaue me and forsake me: yet the Lord will stand by mee, support, and vphold me, in the midst of the greatest of my tryalls, distresses and afflictions, and in due time deliver me from the mouth of the Lyon, for he did thus with *Paul*, when he was to antwer before *Nero*, for his life and Doctrine, at which time *all forsooke him*, yet the *Lord stood by him and delivered him*, 2 *Tim.*4 16.17.18. And I know he will doe so for me too, for he hath filled my soule so full of his

strength

strength, to strengthen me in my greatest tryalls; and of his presence & comfort, to comfort me in my present afflictions, that I know I can liue by faith in every condition, whether in hunger or nakednesse in want scarcity, in prison or in dungeon , or exile or in banishment. And in my present afflicted and chained condition, I haue and do possesse all that my soule can desire : for I haue God & Christ & his holy spirit, and haue rest, true peace and ease, and though I be in bonds & fetrered with Irons, lockes and chaines, yet I am at liberty, for my heart & spirit is mightily inlarged, also I haue full satisfaction, contentednes, yea the world & all, 1 *Cor:* 3.22.23. & for my outward condition, I haue not a troubled thougt about it, for it doth not in the least molest me; for I can truly with *Withers*, in the beginning of his *Motto*; say: *Nec habeo, Nec careo, Nec curo.*
   I neither haue , nor want , nor care for.

When I haue the least, then I haue a feast; and I hauing that, I know God will cotinue it, and for my owne part, I neither long for, nor earnestly desire more dainties & varieties then there is at a feast, and I feast every day; and therefore haue no want of good things, yea did but my enemies truely know in how rich and plentifull a condition I am in, they would bite off their fingers ends, for to heare of my prosperous and happie estate, in the midst of their cruelties, for I haue found and got such riches since I came to Prison, that I thinke the like is not to be got abroad in the world. And of all conditions vnder heaven, in my judgement (a prison and an afflicted condition , for the truth aud cause of Christ , and the testimonie of a good conscience) is the most happie and rich condition : for then Gods holy ones grow in grace and Godlinesse, like tall Ceadars in Libanon, and get great & arge experience of Gods goodnesse, faithfulnesse and kindnesse , as I am able to speake it, by grounded experience. And though my Adversaries are learned in the Phariseicall, Philosical, deceiuable learning of the world *Act :* **5.34.** & **22.3.** compared with *Phill :* **3.5 8**. *Coll: 2.* and haue studdied and beat their braines, in their *Vninersities* and else where, for many yeares together, yet in one sixe moneths, in a Prison and fettered condition : I haue got more true spirituall learning and and knowledge, in the misteries of Godlinesse, then is amongst them all; therefore when they sent me to Prison, they did more for me, then if they had given me ten thousand pounds, for they haue sent me to a heaven vpon earth: for so I haue found it. And so farr I am from being overcome, by their vnheard of cruelty (to submitt and make a base recantation, as they would haue me) which they haue & do still exercise vpon me, in a high degree, that I am ten times stronger then I was at the first, and the next act of cruelty that they shall inflict vpon me, will make me twenty times as strong as I am, and the next act of cruelty after that , will make mee as vnmouable as *Mount Sion*; which

 can-

cannot be moved, but abideth for ever *Pfal:125.1. Pro:10.30.* And as the hatred & difpeafur of my friends (which is the greater tryall of the two) which I haue incurred from them by reafon of my judgment and Confcience, I will carrie my felfe by the help & affiftance of my God, like an innocent & harmeleffe lamb of Chrift; yet will I never in the leaft, either for their love or difpleafure, forfake or renounce the leaft Truth, that the Lord in great mercy hath manifefted and made known unto me, fince I came to prifon. For before I was not only a Novice, but a very Idiot in the right wayes of God, having muddy affections, but wanted inward principles, having fiery zeale, but it was without grounded fpirituall knowledge; But now the Lord hath made knowne to me, by his fpirit, the way wherein to ferve and worfhip him; And he hath made me by his power and ftrength as unmoveable as an Iron Pillar, or a Brazen Wall; And if they doe not in matters of Religion returne unto me, I fhall I hope fullfill that command of God given unto *Ieremy in the* 15.Chapt:19. that I fhall not in the leaft returne unto any of them, though I be ever accounted by them as an allien and ftranger to them.

Againe, I defire to lett you know, that upon the pillary I challenged all the Bifhopps in England to difpute with them, upon this propofition, to prove the Popes power and authority from the Devill, and that their power, authority, and jurifdiction and calling, in which they ftand at this day, is from the Pope, and fo originally from the Devill as well as his.

But thefe Epifcopall Rabbies, who are Cheife members of the Kingdome of Darkneffe, had no other Argument to convince me with, then to put a Gagg in my mouth, leaft I fhould have fhaken the foundation of their Antichriftian Kingdome, publickly at the Pillary, and leaft the people (forfooth) fhould be infected with my fpeeches, which in their account and eftimation, are no better then fcandalous, factious, and feditious; when as indeed they were the words of nothing but the naked Truths of God, and did not in the leaft meddle with the perfons of any, or with any temporall ftate matters, with which I have nothing to doe and fay unto; And therefore they could neither be factious, nor feditious, unleffe the Booke of God be faction and fedition, which were blafphemy once to thinke; But indeed with the Prelates every thing that is faid or written againft their fpirituall Babilonian wicked Kingdome, is counted faction and fedition; for indeed they have no other arguments, to maintaine their tottering and languifhing Kingdome, but Clubb Law, that is to fay, tyranny, bloodthirftineffe and cruelty; But take that Argument and Weapon away, and then a Child will difarme them, and beate them, and take away their Weapons from them; And then to ruine and deftruction will their decaying Kingdome come, and alfo the Weapons that I exhor-

D   ted

ted and perswaded the people of God, to draw out against the Prelates, those Spirituall Adversaries of the Kingdome of the Lord *Iesus Christ*; was not any temporall sword or Weapon, but only the two edged sword of Gods Word, spoken off *Hebrews* 4 12. And they are more described in the sixth of the *Ephes*. Also the next day after my sufferings, by Mr. *Ingram* the Warden of the *Fleete*, I sent this Challeng in particular to the Bishop of *Canterbury*, and earnestly intreated him, to deliver it to himselfe, that I would dispute with him before all the Nobles and Peeres of this Kingdome; And if I were not able to prove that his calling and power is from the Devill, I would be willing to lose my head. But I pray you, take notice of his great learned Arguments, which he used to confute me, and defend himselfe; which were these:

Let him be lockt up close prisoner, in the basest place in the *Wards of the Fleete*; for so runne the words of the Order; and let none come at him, least he should infect any of the people with his errours, and so be a meanes to bring ruine and destruction upon his spirituall Kingdome.

Oh! Scholasticall Arguments indeed; Alas! poore man, are your eyes so sore, that they cannot endure to looke upon the Sunne, or your back so gawled, that you cannot endure to be touched; it seemes they are, or else you would never have been affrayde to have met a younge man in the open feild, to have tryed out the goodnesse of your cause, who desires no other Weapons against you but the Bible, the Word of Life, and infallible judge of all Controversies, and the Liberty of my Tongue, to speake freely without any gagging; And yet you are affrayde, and dare not meete me in a publicke dispute; As poore, weake and feeble men, let me speake in the words of the spirit of God unto you, *Ier*: 12. if you have runne with Foote-men, and they wearied you, then how can you contend with Horses; And if in the Land of peace, wherein you trust, they have wearied you, how will you then doe in the swellings of Jordan; That is to say, if you be affrayde of me a younge beginner in the wayes of God; Or if you dare not venture in the Land of peace, where you have the Temporall power and sword at command, to incounter with me a stripling, that never studied Philosophy, Logick, Rhetorick, nor euer was at any Vniversity, to learne any Lattin, Greeke, or Hebrew. How will you doe in the swelling of Iordan, when your temporall power shall be taken away from you, and strange men of great parts fall upon you, and make open spirituall warre against you. Surely, you will never be able to stand, for already your Pillars that hold up your Kingdome, are growne so rotten, that they cannot endure to be roughly handled or touched; And therefore without doubt ere long your building must needs fall, and therefore looke to your heads, and take notice, that I have given you warning

of

of it, least you repent when it is to late.

Againe, upon Thursday, the 17. or 18. of May last, I was had before *Sir Iohn Bancks*, and Mr. *Littleton*, the Kings Attourney and Soliciter Generall, to be examined what I said at the Pillory, before whom I expressed my minde so freely, that they were willing and desirous that I should hold my peace, and laboured with me by fleshly Arguments, as *Peter* did with *Christ*, to save my selfe.

But before them I made this challenge, and desired them to tell it to the Bishops, that I would dispute with them all before my Dread Soveraigne, (whose faithfull, loyall, and humble subject I am) to prove their calling so farre from being of God, (as they affirme it is) that it is from the Devill; And if I were not able to prove it, (or if I delivered any thing in the proofe of it, that deserved death,) I would not refuse to dye, or if I held any errours, if they could by the Authority of the Scripture, confute me, I would publickly recant them. But their Arguments & replicatiō to this my challeng, was: Lay him fast in Irō chains, Armes, and Leggs, coupled together: And let him lye in them night and day; And let neither gold nor money, nor bookes, nor writings, nor any other thing be brought unto him, from his freinds; And let none come to him, to speake with him; And if any come to aske for him, take notice of their name and place of habitation, that so we may overcome him with crueltie and Tyrannie, and make him submit, for if we doe it not by these meanes, he will hardly be brought unto it; And therefore *Warden of the Fleete* looke to it, have a speciall care of him, that none come to have any talke with him, or give him any thing, that so we may by Tyrannie, Crueltie and Torments, overcome him, for he leads away a multitude of people, and causes them to follow him; And he is of such a lofty high spirit, that if he goe on in the way, he will spoyle our tottering Kingdome; And therefore put to your best assistance, to see if by any meanes you can overcome him, to get him to submit. This was the effect of their speech.

Oh! Brave Episcopall Arguments indeed. But I pray you, did ever Christ or his Apostles, or any of his Servants, use any such Arguments, to overcome or convince those that were opposite to them in judgement? No verily; for in the whole New Testament, we doe not read that any of Christs servants, for spirituall things, used any such Weapons, or Clubb Arguments, as these; for they used nothing but spirituall Weapons, to overcome ther enemies; And with the sharpe two edged sword of Gods Word; *Heb* 4.12. *Rev:* 19.15; they fought against their Adversaries, by this and by this alone, they did overcome them; And *Peter* with this one Weapon did strike downe three thousand of them at a blow, and made them yeeld subjection to the Kingdome of Christ; *Acts* 2. And we never reade of any temporall Weapon that they made use of to defend themselves against their Opposites;

D 2   For

For, saith Paul, *the Weapons of our warfar are not carnall, but mighty through God, to the pulling downe of strong holds, and casting downe imaginations; and every high thing that exalteth it selfe against the knowledge of God, & bringing into captivity every thought into the obedience of Christ;* 2 Cor. 10. 4. 5.

These be the Weapons, and these alone of the servants of God; But on the contrary, the servants of the Devill, their Weapons are Tyrannie, crueltie, and shedding of blood, Rev. 9. and 11. 7. 8. and 13. 7. 15. 16. 17. where the Holy Ghost saith, that the Beast (the cheife members of whom the Prelates are) should make warre with the Saints, & should overcome them; & cause them as many as would not worship the Image of the Beast, should be killed; and that none might buy or sell, save he that had the marke of the Beast, or the number of his name; And whether the Prelates doe not in every thing make good this portion of Scripture (for I know some that are excommunicated by them, and that they must neither buy nor sell, nor eate nor drinke with any man) let their constant cruel unheard of blood-thirstie practises, declare, witnesse & manifest; and therfore, Oh you Prelats, you doe plainly shew whose sonnes & servants you are; namely, the sonnes & servants of the Devill himselfe, as Christ himself doth prove & declare who hath given a lively & true description of the childred & servants of the Devill, saying unto the Iewes, who sought to kill him, (as the the Prelats doe his faithfull people & servants,) who boasted that they were Abrahams sonnes & Children ; *But*, saith he, *if you were the Children of Abraham, you would do the workes of Abraham, but yee are of your father the Diuell, and the lusts of your father yee will doe. Hee was a murtherer from the beginning & abode not in the truth, becauſe there is no truth in him, when he speaketh a lie he speaketh of his owne, for he is a lyar and the father of it;* Iohn 8. 39. 40.

Here (Oh you Prelates) Christ doth show how his people & servants may assuredly know you to be sons & servants of the devill; for he describes & sets you forth by two markes; first, the Devill is a murderer, so are you; therfore you are his sonns, & he is your father, for have you not taken away the lives of Gods faithfull people & servants. Witnesse those that went to Tiburne by your procurment & meanes, in *Queene Elizabeths* time, who were neither Traitours nor Rebels, but faithfull subjects, & servants to her Majestie; but only they were opposit to your Antichristian & Babilonian Kingdome, and therfore you caused them to be murdred; and more you would have murdred, but her clemencie & mercy was such, that she would not to the full satisfy your blood-thirstie murdering desire. Also have you not kept others in prison, till you have undone them in their outward estats, & means, that you have made them to pine away with hunger & want; which the Holy Ghost saith, is a torment worse then to be put to death by the sword; *Lament.* 4 9. And

And some have lost their lives by your meanes in prison; And also have not ye, even ye, shed the blood of those three worthies of the Lord only for spirituall things, who were neither Traitours nor Rebels, (but faithfuller subjects then your selvs, as they have proved in their crosse-bill against you) and did write nor teach, neither treason, sedition, nor rebellion, but only opposed themselves against your ungodly wicked Kingdome; The memory of that unpareleld act of crueltie, is yet fresh both in your eyes & eares, the like whereof in any Christian state, where the gospel hath been professed, was never heard of in the world; I know others have had too deepe a hand in, being your assistants, and have condescended too much to your wicked desires; But with them I will not, nor doe not in the least meddle, nor have nothing to say to them, but pray, and desire God to open their eyes, and to give them true repētance for their sin, if it be his will & pleasure, & so I leave thē.

But you & you only have been the originall fountaine & true cause of all the righteous blood that hath been shed in this land or Kingdom, for matters of Religion & conscience, ever since the dayes of your first predecessour, *Austin the Monke*, (even unto this present houre,) who came from the bloody Citty of Rome, *Rev.* 17. with Antichrists Authoritie & Law, the foundation of his & your Kingdome, with exceeding much blood, as we reade in *Francis Godwins Cattalogue of Bishops*, from the 37. page to the 48. And it hath beene by you & your forefathers maintained & upheld by Tyrannie & blood, ever since to this very time, as I will justifie it & maintaine it before your faces, age after age, even unto this very day.

And the foresaid Author in that Booke, who was a Bishop, & one of your owne Creatures, for his booke of Meeters doth in part prove it; and therefore know assuredly, that the Lord will require the righteous blood of all his Saints & servants at your hands, which you & your murdering Predecessours, have spilt in abundant manner.

And to me that am but a poore, weake & young stripling, little above 20. yeares of age, who you have cast into prison, for a thing I was not guiltie off, as I declared before the faces of the Cheif of you; & yet you have condemned me upon two false oaths, in which the partie, as I am able to prove, hath sworne flatly against himselfe; for in his first Oath he sweareth, that I & *Mr. Wharton* had printed *Doctor Bastwicks Bookes* together; and then in his second Oath he swore, that I did them alone; And upon these grounds you have exercised upon me such unheard of acts of crueltie, that the like wherof *Paul* himselfe among all those tyrants & strange Beasts, Heathens & *Pagans*, with whom he had to deale, had never exercised & inflicted upon him, though he was the greatest sufferer, 2. *Cor.* 11. that ever I read off; but only Christ, who for the sake & the salvation of his elect, underwent the wrath of God himselfe, which no abstracted Creature was able to stand under.

D 3   But

But first, in all *Pauls* sufferings, I never reade that ever his mouth was gaggd, but you have gaggd me, for speaking neither lyes, faction, nor sedition, but only the naked Truth;(the space of an houre & halfe) whereas if I had uttered any errours, or untruths, you being (as you say you are) spirituall Fathers, you ought there publickly to have confuted me, in the presence of the people, you cannot say but you heard of it, for two of the Cheife of you were in the Starr-Chamber at that time, being hard by where I stoode.

Againe, the Heathens and *Pagans* would not condemne *Paul*, as you may reade *Acts* 25. till his accusers were brought face to face, to justifie & prove their accusation; but you have caused me to be condemned, and my accusers were never brought face to face, to justifie any thing against me.

And you *William Laud, Prelate of Canterburie*, for so I call you, and will not in the least revile your person, by calling you out of your name; You, I say, know very well, that in the making of my defence before the honourable Lords, I to your face did silence you in the presence of the open Court, that you had not one word to say unto me, but sate downe as it seemed to me, in a great chaffe & rage, your face being as redd as the face of him, whose countenance did declare, your heart thirsted after my blood, and part of it you have gott; but you are never the better for it, nor I nothing the worse for leaving of it, but much the better; for it hath beene a meanes the Lord working with it, to purge my soule from a great deale of corruption & drosse, hath mightily cleared up my understanding, that I have gott a more true insight by many degrees, into the true wayes of God then I had before; for I was very ignorant of them before, the stripes purged out my ignorance; for the eys of my understanding were like the eyes of the man in the Gospell, who when Christ had opened them, did see men walking as trees afarre off; even so, and no better did I, for I saw the truths of God but darkely & afarre off, in a hidden manner; but since that the Lord hath taken away the scales of ignorance & blindnesse that did hang upon my understanding, and hath annointed my eyes with true & spirituall eye-salve, so that I see very much clearer into the pure waies of God, then I did before, for they were hidd from my eyes, but now the Lord himselfe hath revealed them unto me; but know ye that the Lord will one day in flaming and burning fire (if you repent not, but I thinke some of you are past it, *Matth:* 12.31. 32. *Mark:* 3.29.) render you a recompence, for your blood-thirstie Tyrannie, inflicted upon me, his poore, younge and weake servant; But unto him I committ my selfe and my cause, knowing that vengeance is his, and he will repay it one day upon your heads and pates.

Againe,

Againe, *Paul* when he was a prisoner in the Custody of the very *Pagans*, that had nothing but the light of nature, to guide them in the wayes of God; yet notwithstanding *Felix* the Governour gave command to the Centurion, who kept *Paul*, that he might have liberty, and that he should forbid none of his acquaintance and Freinds to come to him, and minister to his wants and necessity; *Acts* 24.23. also when he was going to Rome, prisoner, *Iulius* the Centurion, in whose Custody he was, yet though he were but a Heathen, gave him liberty to goe to his freinds, to refresh himselfe; *Acts* 27.3. Yea when he was come prisoner to Rome, yet the very infidels had so much humanity, courtesy and mercy in them, as not to lock up *Paul* close prisoner, in a base & obscure place, so that none might come to him, to speake with him, or bring him any thing; And yet *Tertullus* the Orator (one of the Prelates Brethren) had accused him for a pestilent fellow; and a mover of sedition among all the Iewes throughout the World, and a ring leader of the Sect of the *Nazarens*; Yet they let him dwell by himselfe, with a souldier that kept him, two whole yeares, in his owne hired house, where he had libertie to receive all that came unto him, *Acts the last Chapter.*

Oh! *Paul*, it was well for thee, and happie wast thou that thou hadst to deale with *Pagans*, in whose eyes I am sure thou didst finde more favour and mercy, then if thou wast alive, and wert now in England in the like case, shouldst finde at the hands of those that are Christians, in name and boast; And say of themselves, that they are thy successors, but are indeed & in truth, the Disciples of the Devill & Antichrist, as I have already proved, for though all the Prelates in England were not able, having no grounded case to make such an accusation against me as *Tertullus* did against *Paul*; Yet for all that have they caused me to be laid in fetters and locks of Iron, in a close roome lockt up close prisoner, from the society of any; Commanding that none should be admitted to com to me, to speak with me, nor to bring me any thing; Also they are so farre from letting me to have libertie to goe and see my freinds, as *Paul* had; That they will not so much as with a Keeper suffer me to walke a little in the prison-Yard, to take a little aire for my refreshing; my health being impaired for want of aire, and stirring my selfe, which I cannot in the least doe, without much trouble, by reason of my Irons; And I have beene lockt up close prisoner about 4 Moneths, and not suffered in the least to stirr out of my lodging; but when they had me forth before the Majestrate; Yea the Warden of the *Fleets* hath denied me penn, inke and paper, only to write a short petition to the Lords of the Counsell, (in the presence of my Keeper) that I might have but so much libertie as to take a little aire in the narrow Yard, in the common Iayle, for my refreshing.

Oh!

Oh! all you Christian eares that heare of these things, stand amaized and wonder at the bloodthirsty, vnparaleld crueltie and tyranny of the Bishops, which they haue caused to be inflicted vpon me, and had no grounded cause originally for to do it, but onely hearing that I set my face towards *Sion*, as one of the Lambes of Christ: therefore these devouring wolves *Math.7.15.* & craftie subtile foxes *Cant.2.15. Ezek. 13.4.* haue hunted and thirsted after my blood, part of which they haue gott and yet are not satisfied; but longe to pick my carkeises & bones. Now we do not read of the like cruelty inflicted vpon any of the Apostles or their followers, in all the New Testament, by any of those (Tirants, Pagans, Infidels & Heathens) that persecuted them, which they have caused to be inflicted vpon me; whom they are not able justlie to accuse, of the breach of the least Commandement or lawes, of God or the King; though I do confesse with David, that I haue secret sinnes *Psalme 19.20.* and with Paul that I haue a body of sinne within me *Rom.7.23.24.* Yet I can say in the presence of my God, and speake the words of truth, that I do desire and labour to be cleansed from them all.

Also I haue challenged them to dispute with them for my life, before the King, to prove their Calling to be from the Divell, and if I were erronious, & if they by Gods word could confute me, I would recaunt publickly,

But their surest pley and infallible Arguments to convince me, was Clubb-Law, that is to say, take him Iaylour, and lay him in Irons, in the obscurest and basest place in your prison, and let the stone Walls and iron grates convince him, for we dare not meete him in the plaine feild, in a publick dispute, though he be but an unlearned youth; And if it be possible, keepe him in darknesse and obscuritie; And if you can doe it handsomely, that the World can take no notice of it, starve him, for we command you to let nothing be brought unto him.

Oh! you Satyrs, Vultars, Owles, and Scritch-Owles, for so the Holy Ghost calls you, *Esay: 13. two last verses. Esay: 4.14.19. Rev: 18 2.* The Roman spirituall State, being that Cage of filthinesse, that holds you, who are, as the Holy Ghost there speakes, a Company of Dragons, Devils, and foule Spirits.

Oh! you Night-Owles and Birds of Darknesse, and uncleanes, that dare not come to show your crooked faces in the bright Sun-shining light and cleare Cryftall glasse of Gods sacred and unspotted Truth; It sheweth & demonstrateth to all the World, that you are a Company of deformed Creatures, and Sonnes of Darknesse, impiety, wickednesse & ungodlinesse; Or else you would lay aside your Cowardly Clubb-Arguments, and come into the face of the open Sunne, that there you may be seene, whether you be rotten or sound, or whether you be true gold or nothing but durt & drosse, which is good for nothing

nothing but the dunghill, or whether your Kingdome be the Kingdome of Chrift, or the Kingdome of the Divell, for of neceffity it muft be one of thefe, for there is no more fpirituall Kingdomes in the world but thefe two. Or whether you your felves be fervants of Chrift, or the fervants and true fubjects of the Divell. But your hating of the truth and blafpheaming of it, calling it the Refuge of Heritickes, as you did in your open Court, at the Cenfure of that worthy Doctour, *Doctour Iohn Baftwicke*. And alfo your hating and bloody perfecuting of them that loue it, doth vndenyably declare and manifeft what you are, and of whom your Kingdom doth depend. For Chrift faith every one that doth evill hates the light, neither cometh to the light, leaft his deedes fhould be reproved *Iohn* 3.20. Truely you plainelie fhew, that you are men of darkneffe, and workers of wickednes and iniquitie, for you cannot endure the light, for it is too cleare & too bright for you, to come nakedlie and openlie and fhew your felues before it ; becaufe you are men of darkneffe and evill doers, and therefore you hate the light; but if you were men that were workers of righteoufneffe, and walked in the waies of truth, you would not be affraide to be tried by the light of it, but would defire to be brought vnto it. And in the former place Chrift faith, *he that doth truth cometh to the light, that his deeds may be made manifeft*, that they are wrought in God ; and therefore to conclude this point, I will fay no more then Chrift faith, you may know the tree by the fruit, *for a bad tree doth not bring forth good fruit, nor a good tree corrupt fruit Math* 7.18. *Luke* 6.43. But to goe backe againe to *Iohn* 8. In the fecond place, Chrift faith, *The Divell abode not in the truth, becaufe there is no truth in him, when he fpeaketh a ly he fpeaketh it of his owne · for he is a lyar and the father of it*. Here Chrift fhewes that the Children of the Divell abide not in the truth, but haue their foules filled with lyes. And whether you the *Prelates* be not fuch, I appeale even to your owne writings, fayings & doeings, the moft of whofe writings are ftuffed with many vntruths, having almoft as many lies in them as pages. And for the vntruths delivered in your Court Sermons, Worthy *Doctour Baftwicke* in the third part of his *Letany*, hath painted out in there colours, yea what damnable Doctrines are there taught (faving fome few) agreeing with the Filthy Whore & Strumpet of *Rome*, as that forenamed Doctour doth proue in the fecond part of his *Letany*, with which he doth moft truely paralel you, that you are in a manner both of one corruption, yea among all the reft he there proues ; that you hold and maintaine that monftrous and horrable Doctrine of *Tranfubftantiation*, that is to fay : That the Body of Chrift, is reallie, corperallie, and effentiallie in the Sacrament of his Supper. And this alfo may be proved out of the great *Prelats* fpeech, made before the honorable Lords, at the Cenfure of the three late worthies. Yea whole Vollumes may be

E made, of

of those damnable Doctrins that you hold, & are not ashamd to publish them to the view of the whole world (*Cum Privilegio*) especialy in your late printed Bookes, By all which you proue & make good this portion of Scripture ; that you are of your father the Divell, becauſe you do not abide in the truth, but ſpeake, preach, write and maintaine falſe lies, wicked and damnable Doctrines.

Thus haue I by the ſtrēgth of my God, a litle deciphered you in a brief way. But it may be, you will be like a neſt of *Waſps*, which being ſtirred will flie about my eares, with your Scorpion ſtings, but if you do, it will manifeſt you to be part of thoſe *Locuſts* (as you are indeede and in truth, *that came out of the bottomleſſe pitt Revel. 9. 2. 3.* of whom the Hoy Ghoſt ſaith ; that they had tailes like *Scorpions*, and there were ſtings in there tailes, *and they had power to hurt men verſe* 10. But be it known vnto you, that I am not in the leaſt aſſraid of you, for I neither feare an Axe at Tower hill, nor a Stake in Smithfield, nor a Halter at Tyburne, nor Whipping at a Carts-arſe, nor a Pillary in the Pallice-yard nor Gagging, nor Cutting of eares and noſe, nor Burning in the forehead or cheeks, nor yet Baniſhment with *Iohn* to *Pathmos*. For I verilie beleeve if you ſhould ſend me thither, I ſhall there finde Chriſt, which by his ſpirit will vnfold the Revelation vnto me, and then I would write it and ſend it abroad into the world, and it would vex you as ill, as Sampſon did the Philiſtims, & proue as fatall to your decaying, tottering, ſpirituall Babilonian Antichriſtian Kingdome, as his Foxes with fire-brands at their tailes, were to the Philiſtims Corne. And therefore as you loue your almoſt ruinated Kingdome, looke to it, and knowe that the faſter you kicke, the harder I will ſpurre you, & the more you fling, the cloſer will I ſticke & cleave faſt vnto you; for you are plants (which I groundedly know) the Lord never planted, & therfore vndoubtedly he will plucke you up *Mat.* 15. 13. And therefore by the might, power and ſtrength of my God, *Pſal* 118. 14. *Eſa.* 12. 2. who is the worker of all my works in mee and for mee, *Eſa.* 26. 12. For I am reſolved come life, come death, ſeeing you by force & crueltie haue called me to it, to ſhewe my ſelfe valiant for the truth of God, *Ier* 9. 3.

I alreadie made three Challenges to diſpute with you, but you are ſo Cowardlie, that you dare not to come into the plaine and open field, but you fight with tyrant-like weapons, namelie: with crueltie. And therefore to ſee whether you haue any manhoode in you or noe, I make & ſend forth this fourth Challenge, to you Biſhops & Prelates, which is this.

That I will (if you pleaſe) diſpute with you all, face to face, before the King and State, for life and libertie : vpon theſe enſuing Propoſitions.

Firſt,

First, To proue that the Popes Power is from the Divell.

Secondly, That your Calling, Power, Authoritie & Iurisdiction, is from the Pope.

Thirdly, That all Gods people, are bound vnder paine of eternall damnation, to withdraw their spirituall obedience and subjection, from your spirituall law and Kingdome.

Now vpon these propositions will I dispute with you all, and venter life for life, before the King and State, vpon these tearmes.

First, That you shall lay aside Club-Arguments, which is, take him Iaylour, and lay him in Irons, and locke him up close Prisoner, and keep him in safe custodie.

Secondly, That the Booke of God, which is an infallible truth, shall be the sole Iudge of the Controversie

Thirdly, That I may haue libertie, without being Gagged, to speake my minde freelie and boldlie.

Fourthly, That I may haue the vse of some books which I shall chuse. And if you dare grāt me these 4 things, if I be not able to proue all the fore said Positions, by demonstrable and vndeniable arguments, that you shall not be able in the words of truth to gainsay or deny thē. I wil be willing to lose my head and life, therefore take notice of what I haue now the fourth time said and challenged you to your faces, (for I intend to send you this) that in the presence of the King and Nobles you will make it good, and therefore if you be not Cowards, fitt yourselues to come into the open pitched field face to face.

Also be it knowne vnto you, that I will at *Pauls Crosse*, dispute with all your *Priests* and *Deacons*, vpon these Propositions.

First, That they are all of them, Servants & Ministers of Antichrist.

Secondly, That in the place and standing they are now in, at this present, they haue no authority from God to preach his word, nor administer any of his sacred ordinances to the peole, nor the people any ground or warrant out of the word of God, to heare the word from, or pertake with them.

Thirdly, That the Church of England as at this day it stands, is Antichristian, both in Power, in Matter, in Ministrie, in Forme and in Woshirppe.

Fourthly, That all Gods people are bound in duty & conscience, to separate away from it, & to haue no communion with it.

All which things, if I be not able to proue against them all, laying aside (as I said before) all Club law, and letting the word of God be the sole Iudge of the controversie; I will be bound to preach a Recanting Sermon in every Citty in the Kingdome.

JOHN LILBURNE.

FINIS.